MW01168444

The Inventive Process

A Handbook For Teachers And Students

The Mentor Ship
A Passage To Learning

written by deanna klein

illustrated by nancy bosch

Acknowledgments: Without the assistance and encouragement of family and friends, this book would never have been written. Thank you: Nancy Bosch, Richard Boyd, Nancy Cramer, Janet Grow, Stephany Hughes, Jared Klein, Noel Klein, Donna Merrill, Jan Miller, Sharyll Modshiedler, and my students, past and present.

About the Author: **Deanna Klein** received a B.S. in Education from Kansas State Teacher's College and a M.S. in Gifted Education from the University of Kansas. She has been a teacher in the Shawnee Mission School District for sixteen years, the last ten in the district's program for academically gifted students. Mrs. Klein has also taught several summers in an enrichment program for high ability students at the Johnson County Community College in Overland Park, Kansas. She has written curriculum for the school district's gifted program and teaching units published by Engine-Uity, Ltd.

Dedication: This book is dedicated to all those students with inventive minds who strive to make their dreams come true.

Table Of Contents

To The Teacher

● ●

This unit was designed to be used either as a self-directed learning activity for one student or as a teacher-directed class investigation. The background information and activities included in this book will guide students through the invention process.

Your students will find out how other inventors developed their inventive ideas and become actively involved in the creative process through brainstorming activities. They will identify their own problems for investigation and develop workable solutions. After conducting patent searches to determine the uniqueness of their ideas they will apply for patents and build prototypes of their inventions. The students will learn about marketing procedures and develop advertising presentations to introduce their new products to the class. Along the way, students are encouraged to seek advice from experts in their field of research, such as inventors, store owners, and market research companies.

As they progress through this unit, your students will use their skills in research, creative thinking, problem solving, and written and oral language. They will develop original products and be evaluated by their peers.

STUDENT DIRECTED UNIT

• •

TEACHER PREPARATION: This unit can be used as a self-directed learning activity for one or more students. Before the students begin their study, you will need to make two copies of the PRE/POST TEST and one copy of the unit for each student. Administer the pretest and then give each student a copy of the unit to work through at his own pace.

The following checklist will assist you in monitoring student progress:

The student has...

_____ completed the pretest.

_____ read the background information on inventors and identified the invention each of the twenty inventors created.

_____ completed the creative thinking activity, ALTERNATE USES.

_____ listed at least ten attributes for each component of a lunch box and designed an ideal lunch box.

_____ compiled a list of problems he might be able to solve.

_____ selected one problem from his list and brainstormed possible solutions.

_____ conducted a patent search and submitted a patent application for teacher approval.

_____ interviewed an inventor.

_____ completed a prototype of his invention.

_____ completed the activity for selecting a name for his invention.

_____ read the information on marketing and created an advertising presentation.

_____ documented his work in a notebook.

_____ presented his invention to classmates and collected PRODUCT EVALUATION sheets.

_____ completed the post-test.

TEACHER DIRECTED UNIT

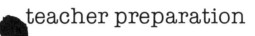

teacher preparation

This book can also be used as a teacher's guide when teaching an inventions unit to an entire class. After reading through the unit, make two copies of the PRE/POST TEST and one copy of each of the following pages for each student in your class: PATENT APPLICATION, NAMING YOUR INVENTION, and PRODUCT EVALUATION. Set up an interest center in your classroom, including as many books from the bibliography in the back of this book as possible. If there is a patent library in your town, you might schedule a field trip for your class or arrange for someone from the library to speak to your students (DAY 8). Arrange for an inventor (DAY 11) and someone from a market research company to speak to your class (DAY 14).

daily lesson plans

DAY 1:   Administer the pretest. Write the names Sylvan Goldman, Earl Dickson, Ruth Wakefield, and Chester Carlson on the chalkboard. Ask the students if they know what any of these people invented. Share the information from the section titled INVENTORS. Stress the idea that all inventions are important, no matter whether they are as simple as a Band-Aid or as complex as a Xerox machine. Assign each student one of the not-so-famous inventors listed on the page titled INVESTIGATE. Ask each student to prepare a short presentation about the inventor, similar to the ones you gave on the people whose names you wrote on the chalkboard. The students will need to use books on inventors and inventions such as those listed in the bibliography. Very few will be found in an encyclopedia.

DAY 2:   Each student will give a short oral presentation on an assigned inventor.

DAY 3:   Present the information on women inventors and Walter Hunt given on the page INVENTIVE THINKING. Divide the class into small groups of three to five students. Give each group an 8-inch length of wire and instruct them to brainstorm as many used for this piece of wire as they can in ten minutes. One student in each group should be responsible for recording the ideas. When the time is up, ask each group to share their ideas with the class. List the ideas on the chalkboard. Ask the students to look over the list. Do they think any of their ideas could be as successful as the safety pin?

5DAY 4: Introduce the terms "serendipity" and "innovations" as explained in the section entitled INVENTIONS. Use the ATTRIBUTE LISTING activity as a creative thinking exercise for the entire class. After explaining the process, list the three main components of a lunch box across the top of the chalkboard. Ask the students to brainstorm as many attributes for each component as they can. It helps to have an empty lunch box for them to look at. Allowing students to piggyback ideas from each other usually leads to more creative responses than they could generate on their own. Accept any idea that would fit on a lunch box. (A stove would not fit on a lunch box, but a hot plate might.) After the students have exhausted all of their ideas, instruct them to select one or more of the attributes listed on the board for each major component, draw a picture of their ideal lunch box and label the innovative ideas they have included. Encourage students to be realistic. One lunch box can only accommodate so many terrific attributes!

DAY 5: Discuss the characteristics of a successful inventor, including those mentioned in the section BE AN INVENTOR. Challenge your students to test their inventive skills. As a class, identify several problems that the students think they might be able to solve. Encourage them to think about the things they do everyday. If they expect to devise realistic solutions to their problems, they must have some background of experience or knowledge to work from. When you feel that their responses reflect an understanding of the type of problems that could lead to a unique invention, ask them to compile their own list of problems on a piece of paper. Give them some time to work on their lists and then instruct them to take their lists home and ask friends and family for additional ideas.

DAY 6: Each student will review his list of possible problems, select one to solve, and brainstorm possible solutions. Encourage students to consider alternate used for a common object as a possible solution to their problem, or to try attribute listing to develop innovations for an existing product. Remind them to keep their ideas simple, and to look for solutions they could actually carry out.

DAY 7: Discuss the information on PATENTS in this book. The students will look over their lists of possible solutions and each will select one to develop into an invention. They will conduct _ tent searches as described in the section on PATENTS to determine the uniqueness of their ideas.

DAY 8: The students will either visit a patent library, or listen to a speaker from the library.

DAY 9: If the students have completed their patent searches and feel that their inventive ideas are unique, useful, and could really work, they will complete the PATENT APPLICATION. Each student will write a detailed description of his idea and make a technical drawing so that anyone looking at the form would have a general understanding of the invention. The students will submit their applications to you for your approval before they start to build their inventions.

DAY 10: Discuss the information in the section BUILDING A PROTOTYPE. Be sure that the students understand the requirements of this assignment. They must keep a record of their work in a notebook. This record should include ideas, problems encountered, sources and cost of materials. The students must construct models of their inventions. Set a reasonable due date for their prototypes to be completed.

DAY 11: An inventor will speak to the class.

DAY 12: Discuss the information included in the section WHAT'S IN A NAME? The students will complete the activity NAMING YOUR INVENTION.

If you want some class activities to use while the students are building their prototypes at home, check the list of additional activities at the end of this section.

DAY 13: Present the information on MARKETING. The students will begin to develop advertising presentations to introduce their products to the class.

DAY 14: A representative from a market research company will speak to the class.

DAY 15: Students will complete their advertising presentations and prepare for THE MOMENT OF TRUTH.

DAY 16: Each student will present his invention to the class.

DAY 17: INVENTION FAIR. All of the inventions will be displayed with EVALUATION SHEETS so that students can examine and evaluate them.

DAY 18: Students will complete the POST-TEST.

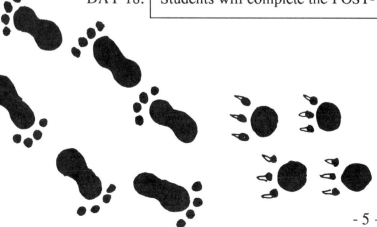

Pre/Post Test

Select an answer from the list below to match each of the numbered descriptions:

Patent	Royalty	Trademark
5	Innovation	Walter Hunt
Marketing	Disclosure Document	Constitution
Name	Chester Carlson	17
Earl Dickson	Attribute	Serendipity
Copyright	Prototype	Unique

_____ 1. The inventor of the Xerox machine.

_____ 2. An accidental discovery that leads to a new invention.

_____ 3. An invention that uses familiar objects in new and unique ways.

_____ 4. Grants Congress the power to issue patents.

_____ 5. Protects written ideas such as stories or music.

_____ 6. Registers symbols or distinguishing features of a products.

_____ 7. Protects an inventor from having an idea copied.

_____ 8. A model of the product made by the inventor.

_____ 9. Used to prove the date on which the inventor got the idea for his invention.

_____ 10. Characteristic an invention must have to be awarded a patent.

_____ 11. The number of years most patents are granted.

_____ 12. Invented Band-Aids.

_____ 13. Involves appearance, manufacturing, packaging, advertising, and distribution of a product.

_____ 14. An agreement that gives the inventor a percentage of the price the customer pays for the product.

_____ 15. A characteristic or quality of an object.

_____ 16. Percentage of inventions that earn enough money to pay for the patent.

_____ 17. Can influence the public's attitude toward a product.

_____ 18. Invented the safety pin.

Answer Key

PRE/POST TEST:

1. Chester Carlson
2. Serendipity
3. Innovation
4. Constitution
5. Copyright
6. Trademark
7. Patent
8. Prototype
9. Disclosure Document
10. Unique
11. 17
12. Earl Dickson
13. Marketing
14. Royalty
15. Attribute
16. 5
17. Name
18. Walter Hunt

Additional Activities

• •

1   Rube Goldberg was an American cartoonist who enjoyed designing inventions to make simple tasks more difficult. Look at some of his cartoons and then draw a Rube Goldberg style cartoon of your own.

2.   Write to the United States Patent and Trademark Office. You might request information on obtaining a patent. The address is:

> U.S. Department of Commerce
> Patent and Trademark Office
> Washington, D.C. 20231

3.   Compile a list of ten inventions that you feel had a significant impact on civilization. Find out when each was invented and construct a timeline.

4.   Research advertising strategies. These are techniques that advertisers use to encourage you to by their products, such as endorsements by famous people. Find out what those strategies are.

5.   Read about a famous inventor such as Thomas Edison. Find out about his life and what he invented.

WHEEL

STUDENT ACTIVITIES

Inventors

Do you recognize the name Sylvan Goldman, Earl Dickson, Ruth Wakefield, and Chester Carlson? Probably you have never heard of them, but unless you have spent your entire life alone on a desert island, you have used their inventions many times. Thousands of inventors, whose names we do not know, created most of the objects that we use everyday. An invention does not have to be as awesome as a computer or a space shuttle to be important. Even the simplest ideas can become clever and worthwhile inventions that make our lives easier and more enjoyable.

Sylvan Goldman invented the shopping cart in 1937 to make shopping in his grocery store more convenient, and also to encourage his customers to buy more. His model for the first cart was a folding chair on wheels with a basket in the seat. His shopping carts were not an instant success. His customers refused to use them, preferring to carry a basket on their arm to hold their groceries. To en- courage his customers to use the new carts, Goldman hired people to push the carts around his store and pretend they were shop- ping. Soon his customers began to use the baskets, too.

Earl Dickson invented Band-Aids for his wife, an inexperienced cook who often cut or burned herself in the kitchen. Dickson worked for Johnson and Johnson and began experimenting with ways of combining the gauze and tape made by his company. The problem was that when the tape was unrolled, the sticky surface would dry up. He finally came up with the idea of using pieces of crinoline material to cover the tape until the bandage was needed. The crinoline pulled off of the tape easily and quickly.

• •

If you like to eat chocolate chip cookies, you will appreciate the invention of Ruth Wakefield. She invented Toll House cookies. In 1930, she and her husband purchased an old country inn in Massachusetts with the idea of restoring it. She decided to make a special cookie to serve in their new restaurant. She started with her favorite butter cookies and added bits of a chocolate candy bar to the batter. She expected the chocolate pieces to melt, but, of course, they did not. The cookies became a great success and everyone started asking for the recipe. Meanwhile, the Nestlé Company had been thinking of discontinuing its semi-sweet chocolate bar because of poor sales -- poor everywhere, except around Boston. The company sent one of its executives to Boston to find out why so many people in that area were buying the candy bars. The company was very excited about the cookies and began scoring the candy bars to make them easier to break. They also invented and sold a special chopper to break the chocolate into small pieces. In 1940, the Nestlé Company bought the Toll House name from the Wakefields and put it on the back of each candy bar wrapper. Soon the company began making chocolate chip morsels. The chocolate chip cookie invented by Ruth Wakefield is now America's favorite.

•••••••••••••••••••••••

Chester Carlson worked for a law firm and his job required him to review and copy many documents. He became frustrated with the great amount of time and money required to get materials copied. In the 1930's, the only way to do that was by photography or a photostat process. He borrowed money from his mother-in-law, set up a small workshop in the back of a beauty parlor in New York, and began working on a method of making cheaper and quicker copies. He was so convinced that his idea would work that he applied for a patent before he had even built a model of his invention. He tried to interest several large corporations such as RCA, IBM, and General Electric in his idea, but they all turned him down. He was running out of money, so he persuaded an engineer friend to help him. In 1938 they made the first dry-process image copy. In 1944 they completed the first copying machine. He named his process xerography, for the Greek words meaning "dry writing." However, he still could not get any companies interested in marketing his invention. So he wrote an article about his new copying process in a magazine called "Radio News," hoping someone would read the article and be interested in producing it. Almost a year after the article appeared in the magazine, Dr. John Dressauer saw the article and called him. Dr. Dressauer was the research director for the Haloid Company, which manufactured wet-chemical-process photocopy machines. Haloid bought Carlson's patent, shortened the name to Xerox, and ten years to the day that the first copy was made by Carlson, the Haloid Company gave their first demonstration of the Xerox machine. By 1959, the machine had become so popular that the Haloid Company changed its name to Xerox Corporation.

Investigate

Listed below are some other not-so-famous people whose inventions are well known. Find out what each of these people invented.

Marvin Stone	Whitcomb Judson	David Bushnell	George de Mestral
Elias Howe	Walter Fred Morrison	George Crum	Melville Bissell
Gail Borden	King Gillette	John Pemberton	Charles Darrow
Charles Menches	Chester Greenwood	Thomas Hancock	Igor Sikorski
Ladislo Biro	James Naismith	Clarence Crane	Christian Nelson

Answer Key

INVESTIGATE:

Marvin Stone - paper drinking straw
Whitcomb Judson - zipper
David Bushnell - submarine
George de Mestral - Velcro
Elias Howe - sewing machine
Walter Fred Morrison - Frisbee
George Crum - potato chips
Melville Bissell - carpet sweeper
Gail Borden - condensed milk
King Gillette - safety razor
John Pemberton - Coca Cola
Charles Darrow - Monopoly
Charles Menches - ice cream cone
Chester Greenwood - earmuffs
Thomas Hancock - rubber bands
Igor Sikorski - helicopter
Ladislo Biro - ball-point pen
James Naismith - basketball
Clarence Crane - Lifesaver candy
Christian Nelson - Eskimo pie

Inventive Thinking

• •

As you completed the activity on inventors, you may have noticed that all but one of the inventors mentioned were men. Do you think men are more creative than women? In the nineteenth century, many female inventors were not given credit for their inventions because the law did not allow them to own property. Therefore, women could not file for patents to protect their inventions or go into business to manufacture and market them. Eli Whitney's cotton gin was actually designed by his landlady and H.J. Heinz's pickles were made by his wife.

A successful inventor, man or woman, is able to think creatively. The best inventions are usually the ones that seem so obvious that when we see them we say, "Why didn't I think of that?" An inventor must be able to visualize many alternate solutions to a problem.

Walter Hunt was an inventor who owed a man $15. To settle the debt, the man gave Hunt a piece of wire eight inches long and offered to pay him $400 for the rights to anything he could make with it. Three hours later, after thinking of many possible uses for the wire, Hunt came up with the safety pin. For this invention, Hunt received $400 minus the $15 debt.

Alternate Uses

How many alternate uses can you think of for a piece of wire? Find a piece of wire about eight inches long. Look at the wire, bend it, let your creativity take over. Brainstorm as many uses for this piece of wire as you can. Write down every idea you have, good or bad. Try to list twenty or more. When you brainstorm, quantity is the important thing. After you have written down every idea you can think of, look over your list. If you have even one really clever, original idea for a product that other people might use, you may be a successful inventor some day!

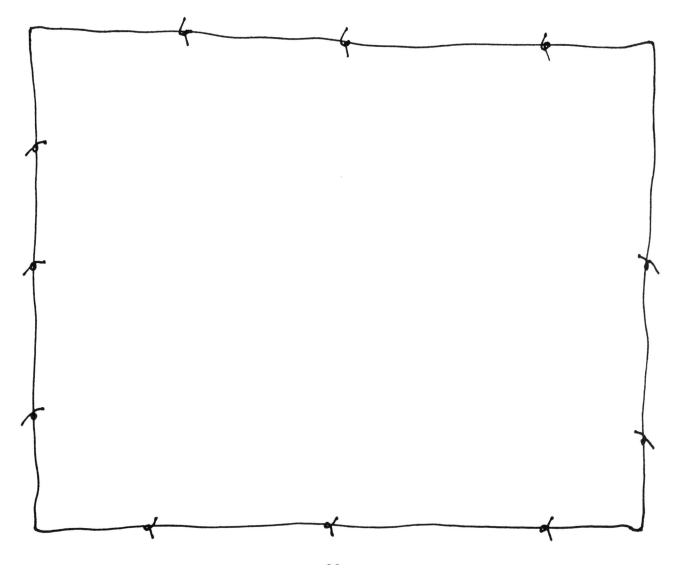

Inventions

• •

Most inventions fall into one of two categories. One of these categories is called serendipity. The inventions that make up this category are the results of an accident. For example, Ivory Soap was discovered because a workman at the Procter and Gamble Company left a batch of soap in the mixer too long and the machine whipped tiny air bubbles into it. The new soap that floated was marketed and people loved it because they could always find it in the tub. Ivory is still the number one selling soap in America. Toll House Cookies and Post-It notes are other examples of serendipity.

The other category is innovation. Innovations use familiar objects in new and unique ways. The Hula Hoop and Frisbee are good examples. The Band-Aid is an innovation combining tape, gauze, and crinoline to create a new product. Magic Markers, clock radios, and televisions all combined products that had already been invented in new and unique ways. Most inventions are innovations. The Wright brothers were not the first people to think about flying. Henry Ford, whom we usually associate with the invention of the automobile, actually perfected the ideas of  others. It was his invention of the assembly line for putting cars together quickly that revolutionized the automobile industry.

Are you an innovative thinker? Let's find out by using a technique called Attribute Listing. An attribute is a characteristic or quality. Most of us, at one time or another, have taken our lunch to school in a lunch box. Lunch boxes are all pretty much the same, pretty boring. Let's use Attribute Listing to invent a new, more exciting lunch box. We will begin by breaking the object down into its main components. A lunch box has three: the outside, the inside, and usually a container to hold liquid. On the worksheet on the next page, list all of the attributes or characteristics of each component. For example, the outside of a lunch box usually has a picture on it and a handle. After you have listed all of the attributes of a normal lunch box, start listing all the attributes you wish it had. You might like a lunch box to have a game board on the lid so that you could play a game with your friend during lunch, or perhaps a battery-powered television set.

Be creative! List as many attributes as you can for each of the main components of a lunch box, but remember this still has to be a lunch box. You still have to be able to carry it easily and put your lunch in it. After you have listed as many attributes as you possibly can for each of the main components, select one or more attributes that you especially like from each list and design your ideal lunch box. Draw a picture of it and label the innovative characteristics you have added.

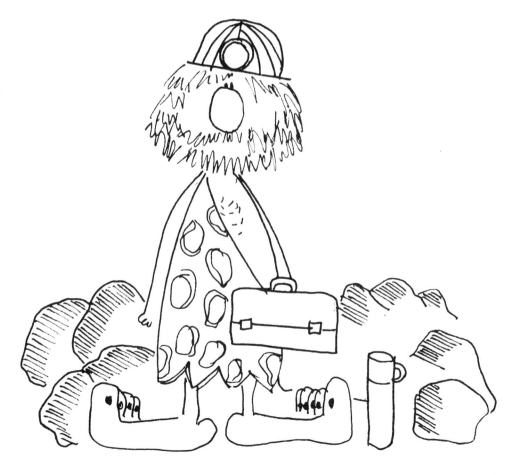

Attribute Listing

The Perfect Lunch Box

Outside	Inside	Liquid Container

Be An Inventor

•••

Inventors are problem solvers. They have the ability to identify a problem and visualize a reasonable, workable solution. An inventor does not give up until the problem is solved. Thomas Edison conducted over 1200 unsuccessful experiments before he finally created the modern light bulb.

Successful inventors can be of any age. Chester Greenwood invented earmuffs when he was just fifteen years old. By the time he was nineteen, he had patented his idea and set up a factory to manufacture his product.

Perhaps you have the abilities necessary to become a successful inventor. Test your inventive skills. The first step is to identify a problem. Think about the things you do every day. Is there something that would make your life easier or more fun? Ask your friends and family what jobs they do that they wish were easier or more enjoyable. Compile a list of those problems you think you might be able to solve.

Select a problem from your list and brainstorm possible solutions. Choose a problem that you know something about. For example, if your little brother often looses his lunch money, you could probably think of some good ways to solve the problem. You have taken money to school, and possibly have even lost it once or twice. However, if your mother has a problem with her food processor and you have never used it, the chances of you coming up with a unique, workable solution are small. After you have identified a problem, write down every idea you can think of. The more ideas you have, the better your chances of solving the problem will be. Usually, the best idea is not the first idea. A person generally does not come up with really creative ideas until all of the common ones have been used.

Try the techniques you have used in this unit. Your problem might be solved by discovering an alternate use for a common object. Perhaps the problem you have selected involves equipment that doesn't quite do the job as well as you would like. Try attribute listing to make it better. Be realistic! You probably are not going to be able to invent a better light bulb, but you might be able to design a better book bag.

Keep your ideas simple. As an inventor, you will need to make a prototype (model) of your idea and explain how it works. Your invention does not have to change the world, but it does need to be creative, unique, and useful.

• •

Problems

....

List all of the problems you think you might be able to solve:

Solutions

• •

Select one of the problems from your list and brainstorm possible solutions.

PROBLEM:

SOLUTIONS:

Patents

• •

Our founding fathers understood that in order for a country to move forward, the creativity of its people must be encouraged and protected. They included in the United States Constitution this clause: "Congress shall have power... to promote the progress of science and useful arts by securing for limited times to... inventors the exclusive right to their... discoveries." In the last two hundred years the United States Patent Office has issued more than 4,600,000 patents. Another 75,000 new ones are granted each year.

Over the years, receiving a patent has become a very complicated and expensive process. Before applying for a patent, an inventor should make sure that his idea really works, can be produced economically, and is truly unique and useful. It often takes several years to receive a patent after the application has been made. That is why you will sometimes see the words "Patent Pending" on a product. If a patent has been granted, the word "Patent" and the patent number must be printed on the product. A person is not required to apply for a patent for his invention in order to market it. The patent only protects the inventor from having his idea copied by someone else. As our society has become more complex, the need to protect

other kinds of ideas has evolved. The Patent Office now issues copyrights and trademarks, too. A copyright protects written ideas, such as stories and music. A trademark registers symbols or distinguishing features of a manufacturer's product.

Inventors usually hire a patent attorney or a patent agent to help them file a patent application. The first step is to conduct a patent search to make sure the idea has not already been patented by some else. There are sixty-two patent libraries in the United States which contain files of all of the U.S. patents that have been granted. The patent attorney or agent will check these files to find out if the invention has already been patented by someone else. If the invention is truly new and unique, the attorney will file a patent application. The patent application requires a detailed written description, a technical draw-ing of the invention, and statements as to why the inventor believes his idea is unique and useful. There is 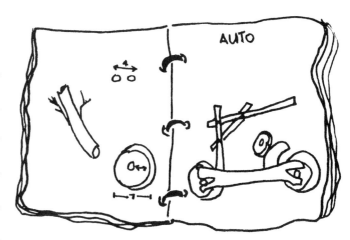 also an application fee. If the application is accepted by the United States Patent Office, the inventor will receive the exclusive right to make and sell the invention for a period of seventeen years.

Most inventors keep a notebook or diary of their work. They write down their ideas, experiments, and anything important relating to their invention. This notebook, with entries dated, can serve as proof of the originality of an invention when applying for a patent. If an inventor is concerned that others may be working on the same kind of invention that he is, but he has not fully developed his idea, he can request a Disclosure Document form from the United States Patent Office. The inventor writes a description of his invention on the form and mails it to the patent office. The document is dated, filed, and held for two years. This Disclosure Document does not take the place of a patent, but if someone else files for a patent on that idea later, the inventor can prove that he had his idea first and obtain the patent and exclusive right to that invention.

By now you should have identified a problem and a possible solution. You should be thinking about a way to develop your idea into a workable new invention. Conduct a patent search to determine the uniqueness of your idea. Check the library to find out if there is information on a product similar to yours. Go to stores that you think might sell your invention and ask if they already carry a product that does the same thing your product would do. If you think that you have a new idea, complete the patent application on the next page. You will need to write a detailed description of your idea and make a technical drawing, so that anyone looking at this form would have a general understanding of your invention. Ask your teacher to look over your application and sign and date it. Later on, if someone should try to copy your idea, you will have proof that you thought of it first.

PATENT APPLICATION

Name: _____   Date: _____

INVENTION DESCRIPTION:

Why is this invention unique?

Why is this invention useful?

TECHNICAL DRAWING:

Building A Prototype

If you believe that your idea is unique and useful, it is time to build a prototype or model of your invention. Keep a notebook or diary of your work. Use a bound notebook, write in ink, and do not erase. Write down the things you do and learn each day while working on your invention. Include drawings of your invention, or specific parts of it. Write down the cost of all materials and where you got them. Sign and date all of your diary entries.

There are several things you should consider as you construct your prototype. Keep your design simple. If a part is not really necessary to make your invention work, don't use it. If you hope to interest other people in your invention, you will need to make sure it is safe and simple to use. It must also be durable. Nothing is more aggravating than something that breaks the first time it is used.

Another consideration is cost. If an inventor hopes to market his invention, the cost of mass producing it must be reasonable. Keep a record in your notebook of all the money you spend on parts for your invention. If you use a spare part you have around the house, find out how much it would have cost if you had bought it. When you have finished building your prototype, add up all of your expenses. Although the manufacturer would not have to pay the retail price for each part, he will have the added expense of labor and, of course, he will want a margin of profit.

As you begin building your prototype, you will probably discover that things are not working just as you thought they would. That's normal. You will encounter many problem solving situations along the way, but don't give up. Remember Thomas Edison and his light bulb! The process of turning an inventive idea into a workable invention is hard work.

To solve some of the problems you meet along the way, you may need to ask people with specific technical skills for help. Before you go to any adult for help, be sure that you have a clear idea of what you want them to do so that you can explain it logically. These technical "experts" may give you some valuable suggestions that will make your invention even better.

If you can find an inventor in your town, call and arrange for an interview. Find out how they work. Ask how they get their ideas, if they have any patents, and whether they have sold any of their inventions. Compile a list of questions you would like to ask before you go. They may be able to help you avoid some problems or offer solutions to ones you have already encountered.

● ●

What's In A Name

In 1908 an inventor named Hugh Moore formed a business called the American Water Supply Company of New England. His invention was a vending machine that sold water in a disposable paper cup for a penny. His idea did not catch on because most towns had public drinking troughs where people could get a free drink of water from a common tin dipper. However, he believed that his sanitary disposable paper cup was a good idea. He changed the name of his business to the Public Cup Vendor Company and began searching for new uses for his cup. He tried selling his cups to soda fountains, with limited success. He changed the name of his company to the Individual Drink Cup Company and again, a few years later, to Health Cups. Still not satisfied with the name, in 1919 he renamed his product Dixie Cups. In 1923 he began selling ice cream in his individual disposable paper Dixie Cups and his business began to grow. After fifteen years, his invention finally became a success.

The Dixie Cup has become so popular that many people call any paper cup a Dixie Cup. The same is true of Kleenex. A product name can become so valuable that the inventor wants to protect it. If an inventor wishes to use the name of his invention as a company trademark, he can put a small TM in a circle behind the product name. After using that name for one year, the inventor can apply to the Office of Patents and Trademarks to have it registered. If you see the letter R in a circle after the name of a product, that means that the name is registered and all rights to use that name belong to the company that manufactures the product. A registered trademark must be renewed every five years, but can be used for the life of the product, even though the patent protection lasts for only seventeen years.

The name you choose for your invention is very important because it can encourage people to buy your product. Buying a Health Cup is sort of like buying medicine, but buying a Dixie Cup filled with ice cream is fun. The name can spark someone's interest enough to try the product, or turn them off completely.

Today, stores are filled with thousands of products that are all competing for our attention. Many inventions are marketed by large companies that hire advertising agencies to devise clever names that will catch the buyer's attention. Modern inventors must have creativity to compete with those companies that have given us Cabbage Patch Kids, Silly Putty, and Magic Markers.

There are several approaches to the problem of selecting a product name. Some products are named after the inventor: Goodyear Tires, Ferris Wheel, and Heinz Ketchup, to name a few. Some inventors select names that describe the function of their invention. Sunglasses, lunch box, hair dryer, and skateboard are all names that describe the intended use of the product. Other invention names tell the consumer how the product is made. For example, ice cream, peanut butter, and corn flakes give us an idea of what we are buying. And still other product names, such as Kool-Aid, project a feeling to the customer.

Naming Your Invention

● ●

Before you name your invention, think about how you would describe your product to other people and then try to select a name that will convey that idea. Brainstorm words that describe your invention under each of the categories below. Try combining words from different categories. Select several names that you think fit your invention and try them on a friend. How other people respond to the name of your product is important. The name should be easy to say, spell, and remember.

Function/Use	How It's Made	Feelings

Marketing

● ●

You have identified a problem, devised a workable solution, conducted research to determine the uniqueness of your idea, and constructed a model of your invention. You have invested a great deal of time, hard work, and probably some money to turn an idea into a reality. The next step is to get other people excited about your invention. That is not as easy as you may think. Remember, it took Chester Carlson ten years to convince a company to manufacture his Xerox machine. However, if inventors want to make money from their inventions, they must find a way to successfully market their product.

Marketing involves appearance, manufacturing, packaging, advertising, and distributing the product to stores to be sold. For most inventors, marketing their invention is the most difficult problem of all. Less than five percent of all inventions ever earn enough money to pay for their patents. For an inventor, there are basically two ways to market an invention: sell the idea to a manufacturer, or start his own company. Most inventors do not have the money or wide range of business skills needed to start a company of their own, so they sell their idea to a manufacturer for either a one-time fee or a royalty. The manufacturer then takes care of all of the marketing responsibilities.

If the inventor agrees to accept a flat fee from the manufacturer for the sale of his idea, he receives one payment for all the rights to his idea and makes no more money from it no matter how successful it becomes. If the invention is patented, the inventor basically gives all of those patent rights to the company. Flat fee payments are based on estimates of future sales of the product and are usually low. A flat fee agreement protects both the manufacturer and the inventor. If the product does not sell well, the company only loses the fee and the inventor keeps the money he received for his idea.

A royalty agreement involves more risk for both the inventor and the manufacturer. Under this type of agreement the inventor keeps his patent rights and receives a percentage of the price the customer pays for the product, usually one to five percent. If the invention is successful, the inventor will probably make more money than he would have received in a flat fee agreement. But if the public does not buy the product, both the manufacturer and the inventor lose money.

Part of the thrill of inventing is seeing the hoped-for enthusiastic response of others to your idea. Most inventors believe enough in their invention to gamble on its success by accepting the royalty agreement rather than a flat fee payment.

• •

The Moment Of Truth

• •

Try some "test marketing" to find out how the public responds to your invention. Design some kind of advertising presentation to introduce your product to your classmates. You might design a poster describing your invention and set up a display in the classroom. Perhaps you could video tape a commercial demonstrating your product, or arrange with your teacher to give an oral presentation of your invention to the class. If there is a market research company in the area, find out what techniques they use to introduce new products to consumers. The companies often have offices in shopping malls and ask shoppers to test products. Be creative! Convince your classmates that your idea is the greatest invention since the light bulb!

In your presentation, identify your target market or the kinds of people you expect to buy your product. For example, if it is a toy, your target market would be children. A kitchen product would probably be of most interest to adults who like to cook. Emphasize the unique features of your invention and estimate the cost of the product to consumers.

Ask each person in your "test market" to complete one of the product evaluation sheets on the next page. These evaluation sheets will help you to identify any changes or improvements that are needed.

Ideally, everyone who sees your invention will be as excited about it as you are. Realistically, that probably will not happen. Everyone who looks at your invention will probably suggest something that they think would make it better. You don't have to use any of their suggestions, but consider each comment. Someone may have noticed something that you completely overlooked that could make a big difference in the success of your invention.

• •

PRODUCT EVALUATION

INVENTION NAME: _____

Rate this invention according to the criteria listed below. If you agree, print a **Y** in the blank in front of the statement. If you disagree, print an **N** in the blank. And if you feel this invention could be improved in an area, write **I** in the blank.

THIS INVENTION IS...

_____ a new idea

_____ functional

_____ attractive

_____ well-built

_____ easy to use

_____ safe

_____ useful, needed

_____ well-named

_____ able to be mass-produced

_____ appealing to consumers

COMMENTS/SUGGESTIONS:

_____

_____

_____

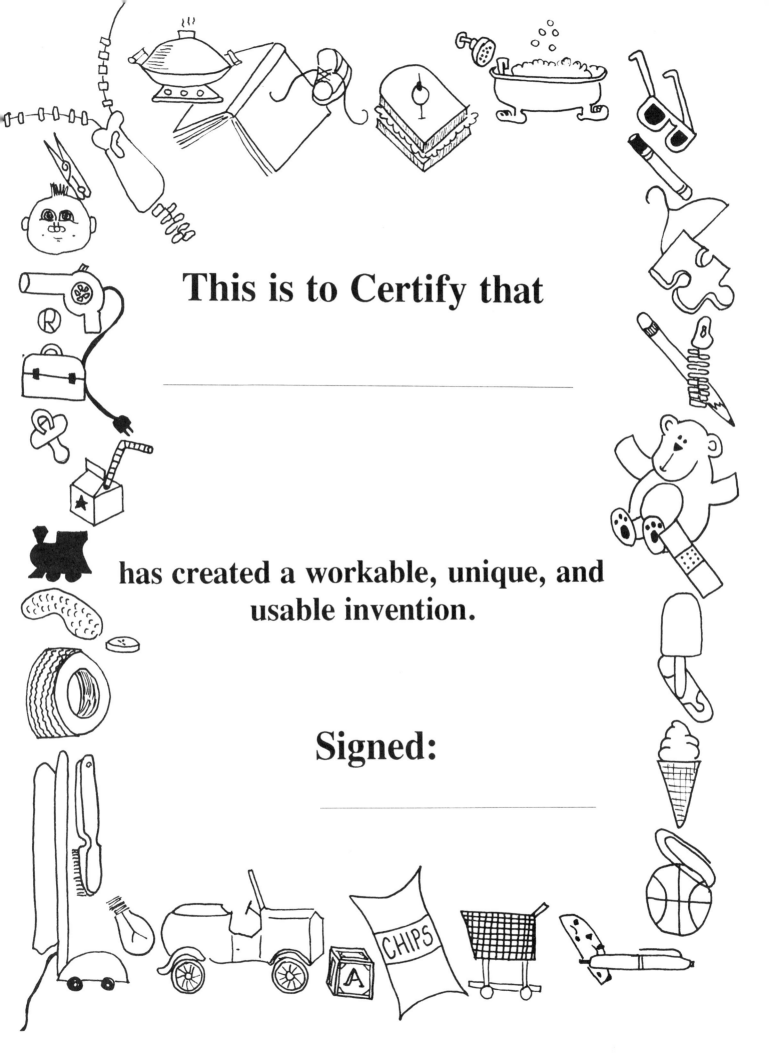

This is to Certify that

_____

has created a workable, unique, and
usable invention.

Signed:

_____

Bibliography

● ●

Butterfield, S., & Sylvester, D. (1984). Inventions, robots, future. Santa Barbara: The Learning Works.

Caney, S. (1985). Invention book. New York: Workman Publishing.

Garrison, W. (1977). Why didn't I think of that? Englewood Cliffs, NJ: Prentice-Hall.

Gudeman, J. (1984). Creative encounters with creative people. Carthage, IL: Good Apple.

Hakuta, K. (1988). How to create your own fad and make a million dollars. New York: William Morrow and Company.

How things work. (1984). Washington D.C.: National Geographic Society.

Invent America! (1987). Washington D.C.: United States Patent Model Foundation.

Keller, C. (1955). The best of Rube Goldberg. Englewood Cliffs, NJ: Prentice-Hall.

McCormack, A. (1981). Inventors workshop. Belmont, CA: David Lake Publishing.

Murphy, J. (1978). Weird and wacky inventions. New York: Crown Publishing.

Mueller, R.E. (1963). Inventor's notebook. New York: John Day Co.

Small inventions that make a big difference. (1984). Washington, D.C.: National Geographic Society.

Spivak, D. (1982). Decide and design. Phoenix: Think Ink.

Stanish, B. (1981). The unconventional invention book. Hamilton, IL: Hamilton Press.

Suid, M., & Harris, R. (1978). Made in America. Reading, MA: Addison-Wesley Publishing.

Taylor, B. (1987). Be an inventor. San Diego: Harcourt Brace Jovanovich.

Vare, E., & Ptacek, G. (1988). Mothers of invention. New York: William Morrow and Company.

Weiss, H. (1971). The gadget book. New York: Thomas Corwell Co.

Wulffson, D. (1981). The invention of ordinary things. New York: Lothrop, Lee and Shepard Books.